THE AUSTRALIAN
Women's Weekly
only four ingredients

acp books

contents

The oven temperatures in this book are for conventional ovens; if you have a fan-forced oven, decrease the temperature by 10-20 degrees.

soups

spicy seafood soup

820g (1¾ pounds) canned condensed
  tomato soup
1 teaspoon dried chilli flakes
500g (1 pound) marinara seafood mix
½ cup coarsely chopped fresh flat-leaf parsley

1 Combine soup, 1 litre (4 cups) water and chilli
in medium saucepan; bring to the boil. Reduce
heat; simmer, uncovered, 20 minutes.
2 Add seafood; simmer, uncovered, about 5 minutes
or until seafood is cooked.
3 Remove from heat; stir in parsley, season to taste.
Serve with crusty bread.

prep + cook time 30 minutes **serves** 4
nutritional count per serving 4.4g total fat
(1.1g saturated fat); 1053kJ (252 cal);
23.3g carbohydrate; 28.5g protein; 4.5g fibre

note We used a marinara mix with mussels in
the shell, but any marinara mix is suitable.

accompaniments

chilli parmesan wafers

Preheat oven to 200°C/400°F. Oil and line oven trays with baking paper. Combine 1 cup (80g) finely grated parmesan cheese, pinch dried chilli flakes and ¼ cup finely chopped fresh flat-leaf parsley in medium bowl. Drop level tablespoons of mixture into mounds, about 5cm (2 inches) apart, onto trays; flatten mounds slightly with fingertips. Bake about 5 minutes or until browned lightly and crisp. Cool on trays.

prep + cook time 20 minutes **makes** 10
nutritional count per wafer 2.8g total fat
(1.8 saturated fat); 163kJ (39 cal);
0g carbohydrate; 3.5g protein; 0g fibre

mini herb dampers

Preheat oven to 200°C/400°F. Oil oven tray. Sift 1½ cups (225g) self-raising flour into large bowl; rub in 50g (1½ ounces) butter. Stir in 1 teaspoon dried mixed herbs. Add about ¾ cup (180ml) milk to flour mixture; mix to a soft, sticky dough. Turn dough onto floured surface; knead lightly until smooth. Divide dough into four equal pieces; knead into rounds; place on tray. Bake about 20 minutes or until browned lightly.

prep + cook time 35 minutes **makes** 4
nutritional count per damper 13.2g total fat
(8.1g saturated fat); 1333kJ (319 cal);
41.9g carbohydrate; 7.1g protein; 2.1g fibre

mini sourdough toasties

Preheat oven to 200°C/400°F. Oil oven trays. Cut 675g (1¼-pound) sourdough loaf into 16 thin slices, discarding ends. Using 5cm (2-inch) cutter, cut 16 rounds from bread; spread each bread round with about 1 teaspoon basil or sundried tomato pesto; place on trays. Using same cutter, cut 16 rounds from 8 swiss cheese slices. Top bread with cheese; bake about 10 minutes or until cheese melts.

prep + cook time 20 minutes **makes** 16
nutritional count per toastie 3g total fat
(1.6g saturated fat); 347kJ (83 cal);
9.5g carbohydrate; 4g protein; 1g fibre

cheese and spinach twists

Preheat oven to 220°C/425°F. Oil and line oven trays with baking paper. Combine ¾ cup (90g) coarsely grated cheddar cheese and ½ cup (40g) finely grated parmesan cheese in small bowl. Place 250g (8 ounces) thawed frozen spinach in fine sieve; squeeze excess water from spinach. Spread half the spinach over one sheet of puff pastry; sprinkle with half the cheese mixture. Top with another sheet of puff pastry; spread with remaining spinach, sprinkle with remaining cheese. Cut pastry stack in half; place one stack on top of the other, press down firmly. Cut pastry crossways into 24 strips; twist strips, pinching ends to seal. Place strips on trays; bake about 15 minutes or until browned and crisp.

prep + cook time 45 minutes **makes** 24
nutritional count per twist 5g total fat
(2.9g saturated fat); 318kJ (76 cal);
5g carbohydrate; 2.6g protein; 0.4g fibre

curried cauliflower soup

¼ cup (75g) red curry paste
½ small cauliflower (500g), chopped coarsely
2 medium potatoes (400g), chopped coarsely
1 tablespoon lime juice

1 Stir curry paste in heated large saucepan, about 3 minutes or until fragrant.
2 Add cauliflower, potato and 2 litres (8 cups) water; bring to the boil. Reduce heat; simmer, uncovered, about 15 minutes or until vegetables are tender. Cool 10 minutes.

3 Blend or process soup, in batches, until smooth. Stir in juice; season to taste. Return soup to pan to heat through.

prep + cook time 25 minutes **serves** 4
nutritional count per serving 7.6g total fat (0.8g saturated fat); 777kJ (186 cal); 17.3g carbohydrate; 7.9g protein; 7.2g fibre

note Sprinkle soup with coriander (cilantro) leaves and a pinch of hot paprika.

pea and pesto soup

2 large potatoes (600g), chopped coarsely
3 cups (750ml) chicken stock
½ cup (130g) basil pesto
3 cups (360g) frozen peas

1 Combine potato, 3 cups (750ml) water, stock and half the pesto in large saucepan; bring to the boil. Reduce heat; simmer, covered, about 15 minutes or until potato is tender.
2 Add peas to pan; simmer, uncovered, about 5 minutes or until peas are tender. Cool 10 minutes.
3 Meanwhile, combine remaining pesto and 1 tablespoon water in small jug.

4 Blend or process soup, in batches, until smooth. Return soup to pan to heat through.
5 Serve soup topped with pesto mixture.

prep + cook time 35 minutes **serves** 4
nutritional count per serving 14.2g total fat (3.2g saturated fat); 1254kJ (300 cal); 25.7g carbohydrate; 13.5g protein; 8g fibre

italian fish and fennel soup

2 medium fennel bulbs (600g)
1½ cups (375ml) fish stock
1 cup (250ml) bottled tomato pasta sauce
500g (1 pound) skinless white fish fillets

1 Coarsely chop fennel; reserve fennel fronds.
2 Heat oiled large saucepan over medium heat. Cook fennel, covered, stirring occasionally, about 10 minutes or until tender. Add stock, sauce and 1 cup (250ml) water. Bring to the boil, simmer, covered, 10 minutes. Using a slotted spoon, remove about 1 cup fennel pieces; reserve.
3 Cool soup 10 minutes then blend or process, in batches, until smooth.
4 Meanwhile, cut fish into bite-sized pieces.
5 Return soup and reserved fennel to pan with fish; simmer, uncovered, about 3 minutes or until fish is cooked. Season to taste.
6 Coarsely chopped reserved fennel fronds; sprinkle over soup before serving.

prep + cook time 35 minutes **serves** 6
nutritional count per serving 3.2g total fat (0.8g saturated fat); 564kJ (135 cal); 6.6g carbohydrate; 18.9g protein; 2.4g fibre

notes Bottled tomato pasta sauce, sometimes labelled passata, or sugo, is made from ripe tomatoes that have been pureed and sieved to remove the skin and seeds. It's sold in bottles in supermarkets, and is thinner than pasta sauce.
We used barramundi in this recipe, but any white fish fillet will do.

mexican beef and bean soup

500g (1-pound) piece beef skirt steak
800g (1½ pounds) canned crushed tomatoes
35g (1¼ ounces) packet taco seasoning
420g (13 ounces) canned red kidney beans,
  rinsed, drained

1 Combine beef, 2 litres (8 cups) water, undrained tomatoes and taco seasoning in large saucepan; bring to the boil. Reduce heat; simmer, covered, 1 hour. Uncover; simmer, 1 hour.
2 Remove beef to medium bowl; using two forks, shred beef coarsely.
3 Return beef to pan with beans; bring to the boil. Remove from heat; season to taste.

prep + cook time 2 hours 15 minutes serves 4
nutritional count per serving 6.9g total fat
(2.7g saturated fat); 1241kJ (297 cal);
20.2g carbohydrate; 33.9g protein; 7.9g fibre

note Beef skirt steak is a coarse-grained cut of meat, which, after long, slow cooking, becomes extremely tender and easy to shred into thin strands for this soup.

coconut, pumpkin and eggplant soup

½ cup (150g) laksa paste
4 baby eggplants (240g), sliced thinly
1kg (2 pounds) canned pumpkin soup
1 cup (250ml) coconut cream

1 Stir paste in heated oiled large saucepan, about 3 minutes or until fragrant. Add eggplant; cook, stirring, 2 minutes.
2 Add soup and 1 litre (4 cups) water to pan; bring to the boil. Reduce heat; simmer, uncovered, about 15 minutes or until eggplant is tender.
3 Add coconut cream; stir until soup is hot. Season to taste.

prep + cook time 30 minutes **serves** 4
nutritional count per serving 27.8g total fat (12.7g saturated fat); 1659kJ (397 cal); 23.4g carbohydrate; 8.4g protein; 11.8g fibre

spicy moroccan soup

1½ cups (300g) dried soup mix
1 bunch coriander (cilantro)
2 tablespoons harissa paste
430g (14 ounces) canned condensed tomato soup

1 Rinse soup mix in strainer under cold water until water runs clear; drain.
2 Wash and dry coriander. Remove leaves from bunch; you will need 1 cup loosely packed leaves. Chop some of the roots and stems finely; you will need 2 teaspoons of this mixture.
3 Stir harissa paste and coriander root and stem mixture in heated oiled large saucepan, about 3 minutes or until fragrant.
4 Add soup mix, tomato soup and 2 litres (8 cups) water to pan; bring to the boil. Reduce heat; simmer, uncovered, about 30 minutes or until soup mix is tender. Remove from heat; stir in coriander leaves. Season to taste.

prep + cook time 35 minutes **serves** 4
nutritional count per serving 3.3g total fat
(0.5g saturated fat); 1225kJ (293 cal);
39.8g carbohydrate; 19.3g protein; 12.8g fibre

note Dried soup mix is a combination of split peas and lentils. It is available in supermarkets.

eggs

egg and coleslaw double-decker sandwiches

5 eggs
½ cup (150g) aïoli
200g (6½ ounces) ready-made dry coleslaw
  (see notes)
12 slices mixed grain bread (540g)

1 Place eggs in medium saucepan; cover with water. Bring to the boil; boil 5 minutes. Drain eggs; under cold water until cool. Peel eggs and discard shells; chop eggs coarsely.
2 Combine egg and 2 tablespoons of aïoli in medium bowl; season to taste. Combine coleslaw and remaining aïoli in another medium bowl; season to taste.

3 Spread 4 bread slices with coleslaw mixture; top with 4 slices bread. Spread bread with egg mixture, then top with remaining bread.
4 Cut sandwiches in half, push a long toothpick into each sandwich to hold them together.

prep + cook time 15 minutes makes 4
nutritional count per sandwich 21.9g total fat (3.9g saturated fat); 2324kJ (556 cal); 64.8g carbohydrate; 21g protein; 8.1g fibre

notes Dry coleslaw is coleslaw without dressing. Aïoli is a garlic mayonnaise and is available in supermarkets and delicatessens; mayonnaise or dijonnaise can be used instead.
To keep sandwiches moist, cover them with damp absorbent paper.

pies & tarts

blue cheese quiche

Preheat oven to 180°C/350°F. Grease 26cm (9½-inch) round loose-based flan tin. Place two sheets shortcrust pastry on top of each other, roll gently to make large enough to line tin. Lift pastry into tin; press into side, trim edge. Line pastry with baking paper and dried beans or rice. Place tin on oven tray; bake 10 minutes. Remove paper and beans; bake a further 10 minutes. Combine 5 eggs and 1¼ cups (310ml) pouring cream in large bowl; season. Pour into pastry shell; sprinkle with 150g (5 ounces) crumbled soft blue cheese. Reduce oven to 160°C/325°F. Bake quiche about 30 minutes or until filling is set.

prep + cook time 55 minutes **serves** 4
nutritional count per serving 76.5g total fat (44.4g saturated fat); 3900kJ (933 cal); 39.4g carbohydrate; 23.9g protein; 1.5g fibre

chicken and vegie pastries

Preheat oven to 200°C/400°F. Combine 1½ cups (240g) shredded barbecued chicken, 1½ cups (120g) frozen peas, corn and carrot mix and 1 cup (120g) coarsely grated cheddar cheese in large bowl. Cut 3 sheets shortcrust pastry into four squares each. Divide chicken mixture between pastry squares; fold pastry over to make triangles and to enclose filling, seal edges of pastry by pressing with a fork. Place pastries on baking-paper-lined oven tray. Bake about 25 minutes or until browned.

prep + cook time 40 minutes **makes** 12
nutritional count per pastry 17.9g total fat (9.1g saturated fat); 1183kJ (283 cal); 19.6g carbohydrate; 10.4g protein; 1.6g fibre

chicken-spinach rolls

Preheat oven to 200°C/400°F. Heat large frying pan on high; cook 200g (6½ ounces) baby spinach until wilted. When cool enough to handle, squeeze excess moisture from spinach; chop coarsely. Combine spinach, 400g (13 ounces) minced (ground) chicken and ¾ cup creamed corn in large bowl; season. Halve 2 sheets shortcrust pastry. Spoon a quarter of the chicken mixture down long edge of pastry. Roll to enclose filling; cut into three pieces. Repeat with remaining pastry and chicken mixture. Place rolls on baking-paper-lined oven tray; bake about 30 minutes or until browned.

prep + cook time 45 minutes **makes** 12
nutritional count per roll 10.5g total fat
(4.8g saturated fat); 803kJ (192 cal);
15.1g carbohydrate; 8.9g protein; 1.5g fibre

tomato-rocket tarts

Preheat oven to 180°C/350°F. Line oven trays with baking paper. Cut 2 sheets shortcrust pastry into four squares each; place on trays. Fold edges of pastry over to form a 5mm (¼-inch) border; prick pastry bases with fork. Bake about 15 minutes or until crisp. Combine 250g (8 ounces) sliced baby tomatoes, 50g (1½ ounces) baby rocket (arugula) leaves and 1½ tablespoons balsamic dressing in large bowl. Top warm pastries with tomato mixture.

prep + cook time 20 minutes **makes** 8
nutritional count per tart 12.7g total fat
(6.2g saturated fat); 861kJ (206 cal);
19.6g carbohydrate; 3g protein; 1.4g fibre

poached eggs with polenta and mushrooms

1 cup (170g) instant polenta
½ cup (40g) finely grated parmesan cheese
500g (1 pound) mixed mushrooms, sliced thickly
4 eggs

1 Bring 1 litre (4 cups) water to the boil in large saucepan. Stir in polenta; cook, stirring, over low heat about 5 minutes or until smooth. Remove from heat, stir in cheese; season to taste. Cover to keep warm.
2 Heat oiled large frying pan over high heat; cook mushrooms, stirring until browned lightly. Season to taste.
3 Meanwhile, half-fill large deep frying pan with salted water; bring to the boil. Reduce to a simmer; create a swirl using a wooden spoon. One at a time, break eggs into centre of swirl. Cover pan, turn off heat; stand 3 minutes or until white is opaque. Using a slotted spoon, remove eggs from pan; rest spoon on absorbent paper.
4 Serve polenta topped with mushrooms and poached eggs.

prep + cook time 15 minutes serves 4
nutritional count per serving 11.7g total fat
(4.2g saturated fat); 1325kJ (317 cal);
31.3g carbohydrate; 19.3g protein; 4.4g fibre

note Polenta tends to become firmer as it stands; stir in a little extra boiling water if you prefer a softer texture.

spaghetti carbonara

375g (12 ounces) spaghetti
7 eggs
150g (5 ounces) pancetta, sliced finely
½ cup (40g) finely grated parmesan cheese

1 Cook pasta in large saucepan of boiling water until tender. Drain pasta; return to pan.
2 Meanwhile, lightly beat 3 eggs in small bowl until combined. Separate remaining 4 eggs, reserving 4 half shells. Return egg yolks to reserved shells.
3 Heat oiled medium frying pan over medium heat; cook pancetta until crisp. Add pancetta and any cooking oil in pan to pasta; gently stir over low heat until coated. Remove from heat. Stir in beaten eggs and cheese; season to taste.
4 Divide pasta between shallow bowls; top with half shells with egg yolks. Each person pours the egg yolk over the hot pasta and stirs it through.

prep + cook time 30 minutes **serves** 4
nutritional count per serving 19.9g total fat (7.2g saturated fat); 2358kJ (564 cal); 64.3g carbohydrate; 29.8g protein; 3.1g fibre

serving suggestion Serve with a green leafy salad.
notes Return each egg yolk to reserved shell half as you break it. Don't worry if the yolk breaks, it still looks nice sitting in the egg shell.
Refrigerate the egg whites and use to make a pavlova, meringues or an egg-white omelette. If not using within 2 days, freeze egg whites in a small container.

pea, corn and bacon frittata

3 bacon slices (150g), cut into strips
8 eggs
1½ cups (225g) frozen peas and corn
¼ cup (60ml) milk

1 Cook bacon in heated oiled medium frying pan until crisp; remove from pan.
2 Lightly beat eggs in large bowl, stir in vegetables and milk; season. Heat same cleaned pan over medium heat, add egg mixture; top with bacon, cook over low heat about 10 minutes or until base sets.
3 Meanwhile, preheat griller (broiler). Grill frittata about 2 minutes or until browned.

prep + cook time 25 minutes **serves** 4
nutritional count per serving 16.1g total fat (5.3g saturated fat); 1175kJ (281 cal); 6.7g carbohydrate; 26.3g protein; 3g fibre

notes If your frying pan doesn't have a heatproof handle, wrap the handle in several layers of foil to protect it during the grilling of the frittata.
If you like, cook frittata in 160°C/325°F oven for 30 minutes or until set. Follow the recipe but combine all ingredients in baking-paper-lined lamington pan instead of frying pan.

fried rice omelette

500g (1 pound) packaged microwave fried rice
10 eggs
1 cup fresh coriander (cilantro) sprigs
1 fresh long red chilli, sliced thinly

1   Heat fried rice in microwave according to directions on packet.
2   Meanwhile, lightly beat eggs and 2 tablespoons water in large bowl until combined; season.
3   Heat oiled medium frying pan over high heat. Cook quarter of the egg mixture about 1 minute or until starting to set. Spoon a quarter of the hot rice along centre of omelette. Fold omelette into three; slide onto warm plate.
4   Repeat with remaining egg mixture and rice to make 4 omelettes. Sprinkle with coriander and chilli.

prep + cook time 15 minutes **serves** 4
nutritional count per serving 29.6g total fat (8.6g saturated fat); 2077kJ (497 cal); 32.1g carbohydrate; 25.4g protein; 1.9g fibre

notes Serve with chilli sauce and lime wedges, if you like. Microwave fried rice is a commercially prepared mixture of egg, ham, vegetables and rice. It is available from supermarkets; you can make your own fried rice if you prefer.

portuguese steaks

500g (1 pound) frozen shoestring fries
4 cloves garlic, sliced thinly
4 porterhouse steaks (600g)
4 eggs

1 Preheat oven to 230°C/450°F. Heat large oven tray in oven for 5 minutes, place fries, in single layer on tray; cook fries about 15 minutes or until crisp.
2 Meanwhile, cook garlic in oiled large frying pan, over low heat, about 8 minutes or until soft and golden. Remove from pan.
3 Cook steaks in same pan over high heat. Remove from pan; cover steaks to keep warm.
4 Return garlic to pan; add ¼ cup (60ml) water. Bring to the boil, stirring, boil, uncovered about 1 minute or until liquid is reduced to 1 tablespoon. Pour garlic sauce into small jug.
5 Break eggs into same heated pan; cook eggs, over medium heat, until egg white is set.
6 Spoon garlic sauce over steaks; serve with fried eggs and fries.

prep + cook time 30 minutes **serves** 4
nutritional count per serving 29.2g total fat (10.2g saturated fat); 2834kJ (678 cal); 56.1g carbohydrate; 44.3g protein; 6.3g fibre

serving suggestion Serve with a green salad.
note Thinly cut shoestring fries are also known as french fries. They are found in the freezer section of most supermarkets.

pasta, grains & pulses

creamy macaroni cheese

375g (12 ounces) curly pasta or macaroni
2¼ cups (560ml) pouring cream
1½ cups (180g) coarsely grated cheddar cheese
2 tablespoons coarsely chopped fresh
  flat-leaf parsley

1 Cook pasta in large saucepan of boiling water, until tender; drain. Cover to keep warm.
2 Bring cream to the boil in same pan. Reduce heat; stir in cheese, stir over heat, until smooth.
3 Return pasta to pan with parsley; stir gently to combine. Season to taste.

prep + cook time 20 minutes **serves** 4
nutritional count per serving 76.8g total fat (49.9g saturated fat); 4431kJ (1060 cal); 68g carbohydrate; 24.7g protein; 3.2g fibre

note Any shape of small pasta can be used instead of the curly pasta in this recipe.

fast rice

chicken fried rice

beef and rice rissoles

Stir-fry 1kg (2 pounds) diced chicken thigh fillets, in batches, in heated oiled wok, until cooked. Return chicken to wok with 4 cups leftover or store-bought cold fried rice, 4 thinly sliced green onions (scallions) and ¼ cup (60ml) light soy sauce; stir-fry until hot. Serve with sweet chilli sauce if you like.

prep + cook time 15 minutes **serves** 4
nutritional count per serving 28.2g total fat (8.7g saturated fat); 2286kJ (547 cal); 21.9g carbohydrate; 50.6g protein; 0.9g fibre

Combine 500g (1 pound) minced (ground) beef, 1 cup (150g) cold cooked white rice, 2 tablespoons tomato paste and 1 egg in medium bowl; season. Shape mince mixture into eight rissoles. Cook rissoles, in batches, in heated oiled large frying pan until browned all over and cooked through. Serve with chilli jam or tomato sauce if you like.

prep + cook time 15 minutes **makes** 8
nutritional count per rissole 6.1g total fat (2.6g saturated fat); 577kJ (138 cal); 6.5g carbohydrate; 14.1g protein; 0.3g fibre

capsicum, goat's cheese and rice frittata

Combine 1½ cups (225g) cold cooked white rice, ½ cup coarsely chopped drained char-grilled capsicum, 8 lightly beaten eggs, 60g (2 ounces) crumbled goat's cheese and ¼ cup (60ml) cold water in large bowl; season. Pour mixture into heated oiled frying pan with heatproof handle (base measures 20cm/8 inches); cover loosely with foil, cook over low heat 15 minutes. Preheat griller (broiler). Uncover frittata, sprinkle with extra 60g (2 ounces) crumbled goat's cheese. Cook frittata under grill about 5 minutes or until set and browned lightly. Stand 5 minutes before serving.

prep + cook time 25 minutes **serves** 6
nutritional count per serving 12.4g total fat (4.7g saturated fat); 911kJ (218 cal); 12.7g carbohydrate; 13.9g protein; 0.4g fibre

fluffy creamed corn cakes

Combine 420g (13 ounces) canned creamed corn, 1 egg, ½ cup (75g) plain (all-purpose) flour and 1 cup (150g) cold cooked white rice in medium bowl; season. Pour ¼ cup corn mixture into heated well-oiled large frying pan; cook until browned on both sides and heated through. Cover to keep warm. Repeat with remaining batter.

prep + cook time 15 minutes **makes** 8
nutritional count per corn cake 2.5g total fat (0.5g saturated fat); 531kJ (127 cal); 21.4g carbohydrate; 3.5g protein; 2.2g fibre

rocket, chilli and lemon spaghetti

⅓ cup (80ml) lemon-infused olive oil
1 fresh long red chilli, chopped finely
375g (12 ounces) spaghetti
80g baby rocket (arugula) leaves, chopped coarsely

1 Combine oil and chilli in small frying pan; heat gently, for about 8 minutes or until hot.
2 Meanwhile, cook pasta in large saucepan of boiling water until tender. Drain, reserve ⅓ cup (80ml) of the cooking liquid.
3 Return pasta to pan with the chilli oil, reserved cooking liquid and rocket; stir gently to combine. Season to taste. Serve with lemon wedges if you like.

prep + cook time 15 minutes serves 4
nutritional count per serving 19.4g total fat (2.8g saturated fat); 2031kJ (486 cal); 64.6g carbohydrate; 11.2g protein; 3.6g fibre

note Garlic-infused olive oil could be used instead of the lemon-infused oil in this recipe.

pea, semi-dried tomato and bocconcini pasta

375g (12 ounces) penne pasta
1 cup (160g) frozen or fresh shelled peas
340g (11 ounces) bottled semi-dried
  tomatoes in oil
4 bocconcini cheese (240g), torn

1 Cook pasta in large saucepan of boiling water
until tender. Add peas, return to the boil. Drain,
reserving ⅓ cup (80ml) of the cooking liquid.
2 Meanwhile, drain tomatoes, reserve
2 tablespoons of the oil.

3 Return pasta and peas to pan with reserved
cooking liquid, tomatoes, reserved oil and cheese;
stir gently to combine. Season to taste.

prep + cook time 15 minutes **serves** 4
nutritional count per serving 22.4g total fat
(7.9g saturated fat); 2776kJ (664 cal);
81.3g carbohydrate; 28.3g protein; 9.5g fibre

notes You need 450g (14½ ounces) of unshelled
fresh peas to get the amount of shelled peas
required. Give this dish an Italian flavour by
sprinkling with basil leaves before serving.

bean nachos

420g (13 ounces) canned four bean mix, rinsed, drained
375g (12 ounces) bottled thick and chunky tomato salsa
200g (6½ ounce) packet corn chips
1 cup (120g) coarsely grated cheddar cheese

1   Preheat oven to 200°C/400°F.
2   Combine beans and salsa in small saucepan; bring to the boil.
3   Meanwhile, place corn chips in large ovenproof dish; sprinkle with cheese. Place on an oven tray. Bake about 5 minutes or until cheese has melted.
4   Top corn chips with bean mixture.

prep + cook time 10 minutes **serves** 4
nutritional count per serving 25.1g total fat (12.3g saturated fat); 2002kJ (479 cal); 41.6g carbohydrate; 16.7g protein; 10.7g fibre

note Serve topped with guacamole and sour cream if you like.

tuna and bean salad

370g (12 ounces) canned tuna in chilli oil
2 tablespoons lemon juice
420g (13 ounces) canned four bean mix,
  rinsed, drained
100g (3½ ounces) mixed salad leaves

1 Drain tuna, reserving 2 tablespoons of the oil.
2 To make dressing, combine reserved oil and
lemon juice in small jug; season to taste.
3 Combine tuna, dressing, beans and salad leaves
in large bowl.

prep time 10 minutes **serves** 4
nutritional count per serving 19.7g total fat
(3g saturated fat); 1321kJ (316 cal);
10.2g carbohydrate; 22.9g protein; 4.5g fibre

chickpea, rocket and eggplant salad

320g (10 ounces) bottled grilled eggplant in oil
2 tablespoons lemon juice
400g (12½ ounces) canned chickpeas (garbanzo
  beans), rinsed, drained
100g (3½ ounces) baby rocket (arugula) leaves

1 Drain eggplant, reserving 2 tablespoons of the
oil; coarsely chop eggplant.
2 To make dressing, combine reserved oil and
lemon juice in small jug; season to taste.
3 Combine eggplant, dressing, chickpeas and
rocket in large bowl.

prep time 10 minutes **serves** 4
nutritional count per serving 11g total fat
(1.6g saturated fat); 794kJ (190 cal);
14g carbohydrate; 6.2g protein; 6.4g fibre

pork and cabbage rolls

8 large cabbage leaves, trimmed
300g (10 ounces) minced (ground) pork
2 cups (300g) cold cooked white rice
700g (1½ pounds) bottled tomato pasta sauce

1 Boil, steam or microwave cabbage leaves briefly until pliable; drain. Rinse under cold water; drain. Pat dry with absorbent paper.
2 Heat oiled large frying pan; cook pork, stirring, until browned all over. Remove from heat, gently stir in rice; season to taste.
3 Divide rice mixture between cabbage leaves; roll firmly to enclose filling, folding in edges. Cook rolls, in single layer, in large baking-paper-lined bamboo steamer over large saucepan of simmering water about 10 minutes or until heated through.

4 Meanwhile, bring sauce to the boil in medium saucepan; reduce heat, simmer, uncovered, about 10 minutes or until thickened slightly; season to taste. Serve cabbage rolls with sauce.

prep + cook time 40 minutes **makes** 8
nutritional count per serving 5.7g total fat (1.5g saturated fat); 619kJ (148 cal); 12.7g carbohydrate; 10.2g protein; 2.9g fibre

note You need to cook about ⅔ cup (130g) white long-grain rice to get 2 cups of cooked rice. If using packaged microwave rice, use straight from the packet for this recipe.

lentil and tomato soup

1 celery stalk (150g), trimmed, chopped finely
500g (1 pound) canned condensed tomato soup
400g (13 ounces) canned brown lentils,
  rinsed, drained
1 tablespoon finely chopped fresh flat-leaf parsley

prep + cook time 15 minutes serves 4
nutritional count per serving 1.9g total fat
(0.2g saturated fat); 497kJ (119 cal);
18.9g carbohydrate; 4.7g protein; 4.7g fibre

1 Cook celery in heated oiled medium saucepan,
stirring, until almost tender.
2 Add soup and 2 cups (500ml) cold water to pan;
cook, stirring, over medium heat, until hot (do not
boil). Stir in lentils.
3 Serve soup sprinkled with parsley. Serve with
fresh crusty bread.

potato and lentil patties

1 cup cold mashed potato
400g (13 ounces) canned brown lentils,
  rinsed, drained
1 egg
½ cup (50g) packaged breadcrumbs

1 Combine potato, lentils, egg and breadcrumbs in medium bowl; season. Shape potato mixture into eight patties. Place patties on tray; refrigerate 30 minutes.
2 Cook patties, in batches, in heated oiled large frying pan until browned lightly and heated through.

prep + cook time 15 minutes (+ refrigeration)
serves 4
nutritional count per serving 6.5g total fat (1.5g saturated fat); 773kJ (185 cal); 21.2g carbohydrate; 8.5g protein; 3.2g fibre

note If you don't have leftover mashed potato, prepared mashed potato is available from the vegetable section of most large supermarkets.
serving suggestion Serve with a green salad and mango chutney.

seafood

spicy thai fish cakes

500g (1 pound) firm white fish fillets
2 tablespoons thai red curry paste
100g (3 ounces) snake beans, sliced finely
½ cup (125ml) vietnamese dipping sauce

1 Coarsely chop fish; process until smooth. Combine fish, paste and beans in medium bowl; season. Shape mixture into 14 patties.
2 Heat oiled large frying pan on medium; cook patties, in batches, about 8 minutes or until browned and cooked through.
3 Serve with dipping sauce.

prep + cook time 30 minutes **makes** 14
nutritional count per pattie 2.4g total fat (0.4g saturated fat); 305kJ (73 cal); 5g carbohydrate; 7.7g protein; 0.6g fibre

notes Serve in small lettuce cups with mint leaves if you like. We used blue-eye in this recipe, but any boneless firm white fish fillet will be fine. If you can't find snake beans, use green beans instead.

canned tuna & salmon

pesto salmon pasta

Cook 375g (12 ounces) linguine pasta in large
saucepan of boiling water until tender. Drain;
cover to keep warm. Add ¾ cup (180ml) thickened
(heavy) cream and ¼ cup (65g) basil pesto to pan.
Bring to the boil; return pasta to pan, mix gently. Add
185g (6 ounces) canned drained salmon slices in oil.
Season to taste; mix gently.

prep + cook time 15 minutes **serves** 4
nutritional count per serving 36.2g total fat
(15.5g saturated fat); 2834kJ (678 cal);
65.5g carbohydrate; 21.1g protein; 3.4g fibre

tuna pasta bake

Cook 375g (12 ounces) penne pasta in large
saucepan of boiling water until tender. Preheat
griller (broiler). Drain pasta, reserving ¼ cup (60ml)
cooking liquid. Return pasta to pan with 425g
(13½ ounces) canned drained, flaked tuna in olive
oil, ½ cup creamed corn, ⅓ cup (40g) coarsely grated
cheddar cheese and reserved cooking liquid; stir
over low heat to combine. Season to taste. Transfer
mixture to 1¼-litre (5-cup) shallow ovenproof dish;
sprinkle with ⅔ cup (80g) coarsely grated cheddar
cheese. Grill (broil) until cheese is browned lightly.

prep + cook time 20 minutes **serves** 4
nutritional count per serving 23.2g total fat
(8.6g saturated fat); 2742kJ (656 cal);
69.4g carbohydrate; 39.8g protein; 4.2g fibre

tuna and tomato salad

salmon pesto patties

Drain 185g (6 ounces) canned tuna in olive oil; flake tuna. Combine tuna on serving platter with 800g (1½ pounds) canned rinsed, drained five-bean mix, 3 coarsely chopped medium tomatoes (450g) and 1 cup coarsely chopped fresh coriander (cilantro). Season to taste; mix gently. Serve with crusty bread and lemon wedges if you like.

prep time 10 minutes **serves** 4
nutritional count per serving 5.8g total fat (1g saturated fat); 936kJ (224 cal); 20.4g carbohydrate; 18.5g protein; 9.3g fibre

Combine 2 cups (185g) instant mashed potato with 2 cups (500ml) boiling water in large bowl. Stir in 415g (13 ounces) canned drained, flaked salmon and 150g (5 ounces) rocket, cashew and parmesan dip; season to taste. Shape mixture into 12 patties; refrigerate for 30 minutes. Place ⅔ cup (70g) packaged breadcrumbs in shallow dish. Add patties; turn to coat in breadcrumbs. Heat oiled large frying pan over medium heat; cook patties 3 minutes until browned all over and heated through.

prep + cook time 20 minutes (+ refrigeration)
makes 12
nutritional count per patty 8g total fat (1.1g saturated fat); 706kJ (169 cal); 14.6g carbohydrate; 8.7g protein; 1.7g fibre

baked prawns with fetta

1kg (2 pounds) uncooked medium king
  prawns (shrimp)
400g (13 ounces) bottled tomato pasta sauce
2 tablespoons coarsely chopped fresh
  flat-leaf parsley
100g (3 ounces) fetta cheese, crumbled

1 Preheat oven to 180°C/350°F.
2 Shell and devein prawns.
3 Combine prawns, sauce and half the parsley in
1 litre (4-cup) ovenproof dish; season. Sprinkle with
cheese. Bake uncovered, about 30 minutes or until
prawns are cooked through.
4 Sprinkle prawns with remaining parsley; serve
with fresh crusty bread if you like.

prep + cook time 45 minutes **serves** 4
nutritional count per serving 8.2g total fat
(4g saturated fat); 986kJ (236 cal);
7.7g carbohydrate; 31.7g protein; 2.3g fibre

note To reduce cooking time, microwave sauce in
an ovenproof dish until hot. Stir in prawns and half
the parsley; top with cheese. Bake about 15 minutes;
sprinkle with remaining parsley to serve.

tandoori fish

½ cup finely chopped fresh coriander (cilantro)
1½ cups (420g) greek-style yogurt
1 tablespoon tandoori paste
8 small skinless white fish fillets (600g)

1 Combine coriander with 1 cup (280g) of the yogurt in medium bowl; season.
2 Combine remaining yogurt, paste and fish in shallow bowl; season.

3 Cook fish on heated oiled grill plate (or grill pan or barbecue). Serve with coriander yogurt and lemon wedges if you like.

prep + cook time 20 minutes **serves** 4
nutritional count per serving 13.7g total fat (6.2g saturated fat); 1308kJ (313 cal); 9.9g carbohydrate; 36.7g protein; 0.6g fibre

note We used flathead in this recipe, but any white fish fillet will do.

salmon and vegetable stir-fry

500g (1 pound) salmon fillets
2 tablespoons light soy sauce
800g (1½ pounds) frozen vegetable stir-fry mix
2 tablespoons oyster sauce

1 Cut fish into bite-sized pieces; combine with half the soy sauce in medium bowl.
2 Stir-fry salmon, in batches, in heated oiled wok over high heat until almost cooked through. Remove from wok.
3 Reheat wok; stir-fry vegetables until thawed. Drain vegetables, return to heated oiled wok; stir-fry vegetables until tender. Return salmon to wok with remaining soy sauce and oyster sauce; stir-fry until heated through.

prep + cook time 15 minutes **serves** 4
nutritional count per serving 10.8g total fat
(2.2g saturated fat); 1279kJ (306 cal);
16g carbohydrate; 29.3g protein; 13.2g fibre

serving suggestion Serve with steamed rice or noodles topped with sliced fresh long red chillies.

tuna and egg briks

12 sheets fillo pastry
380g (12 ounces) canned tuna in lemon pepper,
 well drained
4 eggs
⅓ cup coarsely chopped fresh coriander (cilantro)
¼ cup fresh coriander (cilantro) leaves

1 Layer 3 sheets of pastry, brushing each sheet
lightly with oil. Place a quarter of the tuna into
centre of pastry, crack one egg over tuna; sprinkle
with about 1 tablespoon chopped coriander.
Season. Fold top and bottom of pastry over filling
to enclose. Tuck in short sides of pastry.
2 Repeat step 1 to make three more parcels.
3 Cook tuna parcels, in batches, in heated
oiled large frying pan over medium heat,
about 3 minutes each side or until browned.
Place parcels on absorbent paper.
4 Serve sprinkled with coriander leaves.

prep + cook time 30 minutes **makes** 4
nutritional count per brik 27.9g total fat
(5.2g saturated fat); 1994kJ (477 cal);
28.6g carbohydrate; 27.6g protein; 1.4g fibre

notes Briks are a Tunisian dish. Egg and tuna are the classic filling
but you can also use minced (ground) lamb or beef, cheese and
other herbs. Serve with a squeeze of lemon juice if you like.

whole baked snapper with onion and tomato

4 medium brown onions (600g), sliced thickly
2 large tomatoes (440g), sliced thickly
¼ cup (60ml) olive oil
1.2kg (2½-pound) whole snapper, cleaned

1   Preheat oven to 200°C/400°F.
2   Spread half the onion and and half the tomato
over base of large baking dish; drizzle with
1 tablespoon of the oil. Season fish cavity and
skin with salt and pepper. Place fish on onion
mixture; top with remaining onion and tomato,
drizzle with remaining oil.
3   Roast fish uncovered, about 40 minutes. Cover,
stand 5 minutes before serving.

prep + cook time 50 minutes **serves** 4
nutritional count per serving 15.7g total fat
(2.6g saturated fat); 1229kJ (294 cal);
10.2g carbohydrate; 26.3g protein; 3.3g fibre

serving suggestion Serve with steamed
potatoes, salad and crusty bread.
note To test if fish is cooked, insert a fork into the
thickest part of the flesh; the flesh should flake.

chicken

roasted lemon thyme chicken

1 bunch fresh lemon thyme
750g (1½ pounds) kipfler potatoes,
  scrubbed, halved
1 cup (250ml) chicken stock
8 chicken pieces (1.4kg)

1 Preheat oven to 200°C/400°F. Oil large shallow
baking dish.
2 Finely chop 2 teaspoons of the thyme; reserve
remaining sprigs.
3 Place potato in dish; pour over stock, sprinkle
with thyme sprigs. Roast, uncovered, 20 minutes.

4 Meanwhile, combine chicken and chopped
thyme; season.
5 Remove dish from oven; place chicken on top of
potato. Cover dish with foil; roast 20 minutes.
Uncover; roast a further 30 minutes or until chicken
is cooked and potato is tender.

prep + cook time 1 hour 25 minutes serves 4
nutritional count per serving 30.9g total fat
(9.9g saturated fat); 2378kJ (569 cal);
25.2g carbohydrate; 45.3g protein; 3.8g fibre

note We used a combination of chicken
drumsticks and thigh cutlets.

fast bbq chicken

chicken and basil frittatas

Preheat oven to 180°C/350°F. Oil four holes of a six-hole ¾ cup (180ml) texas muffin pan. Cut four 15cm (6-inch) squares from baking paper; press squares into pan holes. Divide 1 cup (160g) shredded barbecued chicken and ⅓ cup finely shredded fresh basil between paper cases. Whisk 6 eggs and ½ cup (125ml) pouring cream in medium jug; season. Pour egg mixture into paper cases. Bake frittatas about 20 minutes or until set.

prep + cook time 35 minutes **makes** 4
nutritional count per frittata 28.5g total fat (13.5g saturated fat); 1421kJ (340 cal); 1.2g carbohydrate; 20.7g protein; 0.1g fibre

crunchy chicken salad cups

Separate 8 small leaves from an iceberg lettuce; finely shred remaining lettuce. Combine shredded lettuce, 2 cups (320g) shredded barbecued chicken, 100g (3½ ounces) crispy fried noodles and ⅓ cup (80ml) soy and chilli-infused salad dressing in large bowl; season to taste. Divide chicken mixture between lettuce leaves.

prep time 15 minutes **serves** 4
nutritional count per serving 19.4g total fat (4.5g saturated fat); 1342kJ (321 cal); 14.6g carbohydrate; 21g protein; 2.4g fibre

chicken and fig salad

Combine 100g (3½ ounces) mixed salad leaves, 1½ cups (240g) shredded barbecued chicken, 4 quartered medium fresh figs and ⅓ cup (80ml) balsamic salad dressing in large bowl; season salad to taste.

prep time 10 minutes **serves** 4
nutritional count per serving 15.4g total fat (3.4g saturated fat); 945kJ (226 cal); 6.8g carbohydrate; 14.2g protein; 1.9g fibre

chicken burrito wraps

Spread four 20cm (8-inch) flour tortillas with 1 cup (260g) chunky tomato salsa; top with 2 cups (320g) shredded barbecued chicken and 2 cups finely shredded iceberg lettuce. Roll tortillas tightly to enclose filling. Cut each wrap in half to serve.

prep time 10 minutes **serves** 4
nutritional count per serving 14.7g total fat (4g saturated fat); 1304kJ (312 cal); 22g carbohydrate; 21.5g protein; 2.6g fibre

serving suggestion Serve with guacamole, sour cream and grated cheddar cheese.

chilli jam chicken and cashews

1 cup (150g) raw cashews
625g (1¼ pounds) chicken breast fillets,
  sliced thinly
2 tablespoons chilli jam
625g (1¼ pounds) choy sum, chopped coarsely

1 Dry-fry nuts in heated wok until browned lightly; remove from wok.
2 Combine chicken and half the chilli jam in medium bowl. Stir-fry chicken, in batches, in heated oiled wok until cooked through. Remove from wok.
3 Stir-fry choy sum, remaining chilli jam and ¾ cup (180ml) water in wok until choy sum is tender. Return chicken and nuts to wok; stir-fry until hot. Season to taste.

prep + cook time 25 minutes **serves** 4
nutritional count per serving 28.6g total fat (6.1g saturated fat); 2082kJ (498 cal); 17g carbohydrate; 41.8g protein; 4.5g fibre

serving suggestion Serve with steamed jasmine rice.
note Chilli jam is available from Asian food stores, delicatessens and the Asian or gourmet section of larger supermarkets. There are several varieties available, each differing in their heat intensity. Use a little chilli jam the first time you make this recipe and add more or less depending on your taste.

pistachio-crumbed chicken

1½ cups (210g) roasted unsalted pistachios
1 egg white
12 chicken tenderloins (900g)
1 cup (300g) aïoli

1 Preheat oven to 200°C/400°F.
2 Process nuts until finely chopped; transfer to wide shallow bowl.

3 Beat egg white in another wide shallow bowl with fork. Dip chicken in egg white then nuts to coat. Place chicken on oiled wire rack over oven tray; season. Bake chicken about 25 minutes or until cooked through.
4 Serve chicken with aïoli.

prep + cook time 40 minutes **serves** 4
nutritional count per serving 61.4g total fat (9.5g saturated fat); 3724kJ (891 cal); 22.9g carbohydrate; 60.7g protein; 5.5g fibre

serving suggestion Serve with chips and salad.
note Aïoli is a garlic mayonnaise; it is available in supermarkets and delicatessens.

satay chicken skewers

12 chicken tenderloins (900g)
1¼ cups (310ml) coconut milk
½ cup (140g) crunchy peanut butter
¼ cup (60ml) sweet chilli sauce

1 Thread chicken onto 12 bamboo skewers; cook skewers on heated oiled grill plate (or grill pan or barbecue) turning occasionally until cooked through.
2 Meanwhile, combine remaining ingredients in small saucepan; bring to the boil. Reduce heat; simmer, uncovered, about 5 minutes or until sauce thickens slightly.
3 Serve skewers with satay sauce.

prep + cook time 25 minutes **serves** 4
nutritional count per serving 46.6g total fat (20.9g saturated fat); 2926kJ (700 cal); 9.4g carbohydrate; 59.1g protein; 5.8g fibre

serving suggestion Serve skewers with steamed jasmine rice and salad.
note Soak bamboo skewers in cold water for at least 30 minutes before using to prevent scorching during cooking.

cheesy-stuffed chicken with cranberry

4 x 150g (5-ounce) chicken breast fillets
90g (3 ounces) brie cheese, sliced thinly
300g (10 ounces) baby spinach leaves
⅓ cup (100g) cranberry sauce

1 Cut a 2cm (¾-inch) slit in the thick end of each
fillet. Carefully push the knife through the middle of
the fillet to make a pocket, without cutting all the
way through. Push cheese into pockets; secure with
toothpicks.
2 Stir spinach in heated oiled large frying pan,
until wilted; season. Remove from pan; cover to
keep warm.
3 Cook chicken in same heated pan; remove from
heat. Cover chicken; stand 5 minutes.
4 Serve spinach topped with chicken and sauce.

prep + cook time 30 minutes **serves** 4
nutritional count per serving 16.3g total fat
(6.9g saturated fat); 1438kJ (344 cal);
10.4g carbohydrate; 38.3g protein; 2g fibre

smoked chicken and mango salad

2 medium mangoes (860g), chopped coarsely
¼ cup (60ml) lime juice
2 baby cos lettuce, leaves separated
410g (13 ounces) smoked chicken breast,
  sliced thinly

1 Blend or process mango and juice until smooth;
season to taste.
2 Divide lettuce and chicken among serving plates;
drizzle with mango dressing.

prep time 20 minutes **serves** 4
nutritional count per serving 7.8g total fat
(2.1g saturated fat); 1158kJ (277 cal);
21g carbohydrate; 28.1g protein; 4.2g fibre

note Ready-to-eat smoked chicken is sold, in cryovac-packs,
in most major supermarkets.

warm coconut chicken salad

1½ cups (375ml) coconut milk
410g (13 ounces) chicken breast fillets
100g (3½ ounces) baby asian greens
2 medium carrots (240g), cut into matchsticks

1 Combine coconut milk and chicken in medium saucepan; bring to the boil. Simmer, covered, 10 minutes. Remove from heat; cool chicken, covered, in poaching liquid 10 minutes.

2 Remove chicken from poaching liquid; reserve ⅔ cup (160ml) liquid, discard remaining liquid.
3 Shred chicken. Return reserved liquid to pan to reheat. Combine heated liquid in large bowl with chicken and remaining ingredients; season to taste.

prep + cook time 20 minutes **serves** 4
nutritional count per serving 14g total fat (9g saturated fat); 1007kJ (241 cal); 4.6g carbohydrate; 23.3g protein; 2.5g fibre

chicken gow gee soup

¾ cup (120g) finely chopped barbecued chicken
½ cup (130g) thai pesto dip
20 gow gee wrappers
1 litre (4 cups) chicken consommé

prep + cook time 25 minutes **serves** 4
nutritional count per serving 18.8g total fat
(4.9g saturated fat); 1233kJ (295 cal);
15.5g carbohydrate; 15.9g protein; 1.3g fibre

1 Combine chicken and dip in small bowl.
2 Drop heaped teaspoons of chicken mixture into
centre of wrappers; brush edges with water. Press
edges together to enclose filling.
3 Bring consommé and 2 cups (500ml) water to
the boil in large saucepan. Add gow gees, simmer,
uncovered, about 3 minutes or until gow gees are
cooked through. Season to taste.
4 Serve soup sprinkled with fresh coriander leaves
and thinly sliced red chilli if you like.

pesto chicken turnovers

3 cups (450g) self-raising flour
½ cup (130g) basil pesto
1½ cups (150g) pizza cheese
1½ cups (240g) shredded barbecued chicken

1 Preheat oven to 220°C/425°F. Line oven trays with baking paper.
2 Sift flour into medium bowl; stir in 1½ cups (375ml) water to make a soft, sticky dough. Knead dough on floured surface until smooth. Divide dough into six. Roll each portion into 20cm (8-inch) rounds.
3 Spoon pesto in centre of rounds; top with cheese and chicken. Brush edges with a little water; fold rounds in half to enclose filling, press edges with a fork to seal.
4 Place turnovers on trays; brush with a little water. Bake about 20 minutes or until browned lightly.

prep + cook time 45 minutes **makes** 6
nutritional count per calzone 21.4g total fat (7.4g saturated fat); 2149kJ (514 cal); 53.1g carbohydrate; 25.4g protein; 3.3g fibre

serving suggestion Serve with a green leafy salad.

beef & veal

dukkah veal with chilli beans

8 veal medallions (680g)
¼ cup (30g) pistachio dukkah
500g (1 pound) green beans, trimmed
1 fresh long red chilli, sliced thinly

1 Sprinkle veal, both sides, with dukkah. Cook in heated oiled large frying pan over high heat.
2 Meanwhile, boil, steam or microwave beans until tender; drain.
3 Heat medium oiled frying pan over high heat. Add chilli, cook, stirring, until fragrant. Add beans, cook, stirring, until heated through. Season to taste.
4 Serve veal with chilli beans.

prep + cook time 20 minutes **serves** 4
nutritional count per serving 10.1g total fat
(1.2g saturated fat); 1179kJ (282 cal);
4.1g carbohydrate; 41.2g protein; 4.4g fibre

pastry bites

fetta and pine nut pinwheels

Preheat oven to 200°C/400°F. Combine 500g (1 pound) minced (ground) beef, 185g (6 ounces) crumbled fetta cheese and ¼ cup (40g) chopped roasted pine nuts in large bowl; season. Place 2 sheets puff pastry on board. Spread mince mixture evenly over pastry sheets, leaving a 5cm border on one edge. Starting with border facing away from you, roll up tightly to form a pinwheel. Using a serrated knife, trim and discard ends. Slice each roll into 12 pinwheels. Place pinwheels on baking-paper-lined oven trays. Bake about 25 minutes or until browned. Serve with tomato relish if you like.

prep + cook time 45 minutes **makes** 24
nutritional count per pinwheel 7.8g total fat (3.7g saturated fat); 489kJ (117 cal); 5.1g carbohydrate; 6.5g protein; 0.3g fibre

sausage rolls

Preheat oven to 200°C/400°F. Combine 500g (1 pound) minced (ground) beef, ½ cup (35g) stale breadcrumbs and ½ cup (140g) barbecue relish in medium bowl; season. Place 2 sheets puff pastry on board; cut each in half. Divide mince mixture into four portions. Roll each portion into a long log. Place along one long edge of each pastry half. Roll up to enclose mince mixture. Cut each roll into 6 pieces. Place on baking-paper-lined oven trays. Bake about 25 minutes or until browned. Serve with tomato sauce (ketchup).

prep + cook time 40 minutes **makes** 24
nutritional count per piece 4.8g total fat (2.5g saturated fat); 393kJ (94 cal); 7.3g carbohydrate; 5.3g protein; 0.3g fibre

curry puffs

Heat oiled large frying pan over high heat. Add 400g (13 ounces) minced (ground) beef; cook, stirring, until browned. Add 2 tablespoons mild curry powder; cook, stirring, until fragrant. Add 1 medium peeled and finely chopped potato and 1 cup (250ml) cold water; bring to the boil. Simmer, uncovered, about 10 minutes or until water evaporates and potato is tender. Cool. Preheat oven to 220°C/425°F. Cut 8.5cm (3½-inch) rounds from 6 sheets puff pastry. Place level tablespoons of filling on one side of each pastry round. Fold pastry over to enclose filling. Place on baking-paper-lined oven trays. Bake about 25 minutes or until browned. Serve with yogurt or chutney.

prep + cook time 50 minutes **makes** 36
nutritional count per puff 6.3g total fat (3.3g saturated fat); 451kJ (108 cal); 9g carbohydrate; 3.7g protein; 0.5g fibre

pigs in blankets

Preheat oven to 200°C/400°F. Heat oiled large frying pan over high heat. Cook 12 chipolata sausages until browned all over; remove from heat. Cut 1 sheet puff pastry into 12 rectangles. Brush pastry with lightly beaten egg. Place one sausage on each pastry rectangle; roll to enclose. Place on baking-paper-lined oven tray. Bake about 20 minutes or until browned. Place 2 tablespoons dijonnaise into the corner of a small plastic bag; snip the end with scissors and pipe a squiggle on each just before serving.

prep + cook time 35 minutes **makes** 12
nutritional count per piece 11.3g total fat (4.7g saturated fat); 619kJ (148 cal); 6.6g carbohydrate; 5g protein; 0.6g fibre

one-pan sausage bake

8 thick beef sausages (1.2kg)
2 medium yellow capsicums (bell peppers) (400g),
  sliced thickly
375g (12 ounces) cherry tomatoes
1 small red onion (100g), cut into wedges

1 Preheat oven to 200°C/400°F.
2 Heat large flameproof baking dish over high heat. Cook sausages until browned all over. Add capsicum, tomatoes and onion; season.
3 Roast, uncovered, about 30 minutes or until sausages are cooked through and the vegetables are tender.

prep + cook time 40 minutes **serves** 4
nutritional count per serving 76.4g total fat (36.6g saturated fat); 3737kJ (894 cal); 12g carbohydrate; 36.9g protein; 10.3g fibre

serving suggestion Serve with mashed potatoes or soft polenta and rocket.

steak with pea puree

4 beef scotch fillet steaks (600g)
1 tablespoon finely chopped fresh rosemary
500g (1 pound) frozen green peas
30g (1 ounce) butter

1 Sprinkle beef with rosemary; season. Cook in heated oiled large frying pan over high heat.
2 Meanwhile, heat medium saucepan over high heat. Add peas, butter and 2 tablespoons water. Bring to the boil, remove from heat. Process peas until almost smooth. Season to taste.
3 Serve pea puree with beef.

prep + cook time 20 minutes serves 4
nutritional count per serving 26.5g total fat
(12g saturated fat); 1885kJ (451 cal);
9.9g carbohydrate; 40.1g protein; 7.3g fibre

serving suggestion Serve with steamed chat potatoes and baby carrots.

veal parmigiana

1 medium eggplant (300g), cut into 8 slices
4 x 125g (4-ounce) veal schnitzels
1 cup (250g) bottled tomato pasta sauce
6 bocconcini cheeses (360g), sliced thinly

1 Heat oiled large heatproof frying pan over high heat. Cook eggplant in batches until tender and browned both sides. Remove from pan.
2 Cook veal in same heated oiled pan. Place 2 slices of eggplant on each slice of veal; season. Top with sauce and cheese.
3 Preheat griller (broiler). Grill until cheese melts.

prep + cook time 35 minutes **serves** 4
nutritional count per serving 18.6g total fat
(10.1g saturated fat); 1593kJ (381 cal);
8.1g carbohydrate; 44.1g protein; 2.9g fibre

serving suggestion Serve with soft polenta and a green salad.
note If your frying pan doesn't have a heatproof handle, wrap the handle in several layers of foil to protect it during the grilling.

beef and mushroom pies

2 sheets shortcrust pastry
150g (5 ounces) coarsely chopped
  mushrooms
250g (8 ounces) minced (ground) beef
½ cup (125g) bottled tomato and basil pasta sauce

1 Preheat oven to 180°C/350°F.
2 Cut one pastry sheet into four squares. Line four oiled 9.5cm (3½-inch) pie tins with pastry; trim excess pastry. Line pastry cases with baking paper, fill with dried beans or rice. Place tins on oven tray; bake 10 minutes. Remove paper and beans. Return to oven; bake 5 minutes.
3 Meanwhile, cook mushrooms in oiled large frying pan until lightly browned. Add beef; cook, stirring, until browned. Stir in sauce; season to taste.
4 Fill pastry cases with beef mixture.
5 Cut four 11cm (4½-inch) rounds from remaining pastry sheet; cover filling with pastry rounds, pressing edges together with a fork to seal. Make small cuts in tops of each pie; bake pies about 25 minutes or until browned.

prep + cook time 50 minutes **makes** 4
nutritional count per pie 26.3g total fat
(13.1g saturated fat); 1914kJ (458 cal);
35.9g carbohydrate; 18.9g protein; 2.9g fibre

serving suggestion Serve with potato and pea mash and tomato sauce.

chilli garlic beef stir-fry

625g (1¼ pounds) beef rump steak, trimmed,
  sliced thinly
1 tablespoon garlic chilli sauce
500g (1 pound) stir-fry vegetable mixture
⅓ cup (80ml) oyster sauce

1 Heat oiled wok; stir-fry beef, in batches, until
almost cooked. Remove from wok.
2 Stir-fry garlic chilli sauce and vegetables in wok
until vegetables are tender.
3 Return beef to wok with 2 tablespoons water
and oyster sauce. Stir-fry until heated through.

prep + cook time 20 minutes **serves** 4
nutritional count per serving 9.2g total fat
(3.4g saturated fat); 1287kJ (308 cal);
14.4g carbohydrate; 37.1g protein; 8.5g fibre

serving suggestion Serve with steamed rice or
stir-fried noodles.
note Fresh or frozen stir-fry vegetables can be
used in this recipe.

veal with sage brown butter

12 fresh sage leaves
4 veal cutlets (680g)
60g (2 ounces) butter
2 teaspoons lemon juice

1   Press one sage leaf on both sides of each veal cutlet. Cook veal in heated oiled large frying pan over high heat.

2   Meanwhile, heat butter in small frying pan until browned lightly. Add remaining sage; cook over low heat about 1 minute or until sage is browned lightly. Remove from heat; stir in juice. Season to taste.
3   Serve veal with sage butter mixture.

prep + cook time 15 minutes   **serves** 4
nutritional count per serving 17.2g total fat (9.9g saturated fat); 1200kJ (287 cal); 0.2g carbohydrate; 33.2g protein; 0g fibre

serving suggestion Serve with mashed potatoes and steamed vegetables.

savoury mince

1 medium brown onion (150g), chopped finely
600g (1¼ pounds) minced (ground) beef
½ cup (140g) tomato paste
800g (1½ pounds) canned diced tomatoes

1 Cook onion in heated oiled large saucepan, stirring, over heat, until softened. Add beef; cook, stirring, until beef changes colour.
2 Add paste and undrained tomatoes to pan; bring to the boil. Simmer, uncovered, stirring occasionally, about 20 minutes or until thick. Season to taste.

prep + cook time 40 minutes **serves** 4
nutritional count per serving 13g total fat
(5.7g saturated fat); 1287kJ (308 cal);
12.1g carbohydrate; 33.1g protein; 4.3g fibre

note This recipe could also be used as a base for lasagne, cottage pie, nachos and bolognese. Serve with char-grilled crusty bread.

veal with lemon basil cream sauce

1 medium lemon (140g)
500g (1 pound) veal schnitzels
1¼ cups (310ml) pouring cream
¼ cup finely shredded fresh basil leaves

1 Finely grate 2 teaspoons of rind from lemon; squeeze and reserve 1 tablespoon of juice.
2 Heat oiled large frying pan over high heat. Cook veal until browned lightly both sides. Remove from pan; cover to keep warm.
3 Add cream to pan; bring to the boil, stirring. Simmer, uncovered, about 5 minutes or until thickened slightly. Add rind and juice; return to the boil. Remove from heat; season to taste. Stir in basil.
4 Serve sauce over veal.

prep + cook time 15 minutes **serves** 4
nutritional count per serving 36.7g total fat (22.5g saturated fat); 1877kJ (449 cal); 2.3g carbohydrate; 28.4g protein; 0.1g fibre

note Veal schnitzel is thinly sliced steak available crumbed or plain (uncrumbed); we use plain schnitzel, sometimes called escalopes.

toad in the hole

8 chipolata sausages (240g)
¾ cup (110g) plain (all-purpose) flour
3 eggs, beaten lightly
1 cup (250ml) milk

1 Grease 1.5-litre (6-cup) shallow ovenproof dish. Place dish in the oven. Preheat oven to 220°C/425°F.
2 Cook sausages in heated oiled large frying pan over medium heat until browned all over.

3 Meanwhile, whisk flour, egg and milk in large jug until smooth; season. Strain batter into preheated dish. Place sausages in batter, bake about 20 minutes or until golden. Sprinkle with thyme or rosemary leaves, if you like.

prep + cook time 35 minutes **serves** 4
nutritional count per serving 23g total fat (10.4g saturated fat); 1576kJ (377 cal); 24.2g carbohydrate; 17.7g protein; 2.6g fibre

beef wellies

60g (2 ounces) baby spinach
3 sheets puff pastry
350g (11 ounces) piece beef eye fillet
1 egg

prep + cook time 30 minutes **makes** 8
nutritional count per wellie 14g total fat
(8.3g saturated fat); 1133kJ (271 cal);
21g carbohydrate; 14.3g protein; 2.2g fibre

1 Preheat oven to 240°C/475°F.
2 Cook spinach in medium saucepan until wilted.
3 Cut 8 x 10cm (4-inch) rounds from pastry sheets.
4 Cut beef into eight 1cm (½-inch) slices; season.
5 Place small amounts of spinach on top of each piece of beef. Place pastry rounds over beef; press pastry over and around beef to enclose, leaving the base open slightly to allow juices to escape.
6 Place beef parcels on oiled wire rack over baking dish; brush with egg. Bake about 15 minutes or until pastry is browned.

sun-dried tomato meatloaf

750g (1½ pounds) minced (ground) veal
½ cup (130g) sun-dried tomato pesto
1 cup (70g) stale breadcrumbs
1 egg, beaten lightly

1 Preheat oven to 200°C/400°F. Line base and sides of 11cm x 19cm (4½-inch x 7½-inch) loaf pan with baking paper.
2 Combine veal, pesto, breadcrumbs and egg in large bowl; season. Press mixture into pan. Bake about 40 minutes or until cooked through. Stand 10 minutes before slicing.

prep + cook time 50 minutes **serves** 4
nutritional count per serving 28.2g total fat (8.6g saturated fat); 2073kJ (496 cal); 11.9g carbohydrate; 48.3g protein; 1.5g fibre

serving suggestion Serve with mashed potato and steamed vegies.

satay beef and noodle stir-fry

450g (14 ounces) thin hokkien noodles
500g (1 pound) beef rump steak, trimmed,
  sliced thinly
315g (10 ounces) stir-fry vegetable mixture
1 cup (250ml) satay sauce

1 Place noodles in medium heatproof bowl, cover
with boiling water; separate with fork, drain.
2 Heat oiled wok; stir-fry beef, in batches, until
almost cooked. Remove from wok.
3 Stir-fry vegetables in wok until tender. Return
beef to wok with noodles and sauce. Stir-fry until
heated through.

prep + cook time 15 minutes **serves** 4
nutritional count per serving 16.2g total fat
(5.5g saturated fat); 2654kJ (635 cal);
73.9g carbohydrate; 43.3g protein; 9.4g fibre

note Fresh or frozen stir-fry vegetables can be used in this recipe.

steak with mushroom gravy

4 beef T-bone steaks (1.2kg)
250g (8 ounces) button mushrooms, sliced thinly
1 tablespoon plain (all-purpose) flour
1¼ cups (310ml) beef stock

1 Season beef. Cook beef in heated oiled large frying pan over high heat. Remove from pan; cover to keep warm.
2 Cook mushrooms in same heated pan, stirring, until tender. Add flour, cook, stirring for 1 minute. Gradually stir in stock; bring to the boil, stirring until gravy boils and thickens.
3 Serve beef with gravy.

prep + cook time 20 minutes **serves** 4
nutritional count per serving 28.1g total fat (11.4g saturated fat); 1885kJ (451 cal); 3.4g carbohydrate; 45.7g protein; 1.7g fibre

serving suggestion Serve with mashed or roasted potatoes.
note Veal T-bone steaks can also be used.

lamb

dukkah lamb cutlets with honey

12 french-trimmed lamb cutlets (600g)
¼ cup (30g) dukkah spice mix
1 tablespoon honey
1 tablespoon pomegranate molasses

1 Dip both sides of lamb cutlets into dukkah mix.
2 Cook lamb on heated oiled grill plate
(or grill pan or barbecue).
3 Serve lamb drizzled with combined
honey and molasses.

prep + cook time 10 minutes **serves** 4
nutritional count per serving 10.6g total fat
(3.8g saturated fat); 890kJ (213 cal);
11.4g carbohydrate; 18.1g protein; 0.6g fibre

serving suggestion Served with herbed couscous.
note Pomegranate molasses has a tart, fruity taste
similar to balsamic vinegar. It is available at Middle
Eastern food stores and specialty food shops.

lamb wraps

mexican lamb tortillas

Combine 600g (1¼ pounds) lamb strips and 50g
(1½-ounce) packet burrito seasoning in medium
bowl. Heat oiled wok; cook lamb in batches.
Meanwhile, heat eight 15cm (6-inch) white flour
tortillas (220g) according to packet instructions.
Serve lamb with warm tortillas and 300g
(9½ ounces) chunky tomato capsicum salsa.

prep + cook time 15 minutes **serves** 4
nutritional count per serving 12.7g total fat
(3.5g saturated fat); 1835kJ (439 cal);
39g carbohydrate; 39.3g protein; 4.3g fibre

lamb haloumi wraps

Combine 600g (1¼ pounds) diced lamb fillet and
2 teaspoons piri piri seasoning in medium bowl.
Thread lamb onto 4 bamboo skewers. Cook
skewers on heated oiled grill plate (or grill pan or
barbecue). Cook 250g thinly sliced haloumi cheese
on heated oiled grill plate until browned both sides.
Divide lamb and haloumi among 4 large pitta
bread (320g); roll to enclose filling.

prep + cook time 15 minutes **makes** 4
nutritional count per wrap 21.8g total fat
(10.2g saturated fat); 2633kJ (630 cal); 52.4g
carbohydrate; 54.5g protein; 2.9g fibre

lamb, fetta and tomato wraps

Drain ¾ cup (150g) marinated fetta cheese in oil, reserving 1 tablespoon of the oil. Spread the cheese over one side of 4 wholemeal lavash bread wraps (230g). Divide 400g (13 ounces) leftover thinly sliced roast lamb and 2 thickly sliced medium tomatoes among wraps; season to taste. Drizzle with reserved oil; roll to enclose filling.

prep time 10 minutes **makes** 4
nutritional count per wrap 23.7g total fat (10.2g saturated fat); 2132kJ (510 cal); 29.7g carbohydrate; 42g protein; 4.7g fibre

lamb pitta pockets

Spread the inside of 4 halved large pitta pocket breads (320g) with 1 cup (250g) baba ghanoush. Fill with 400g (13 ounces) leftover thinly sliced roast lamb and 50g (1½ ounces) baby rocket (arugula) leaves. Season to taste.

prep time 10 minutes **serves** 4
nutritional count per serving 11.6g total fat (4.1g saturated fat); 1818kJ (435 cal); 42.6g carbohydrate; 37.6g protein; 3.9g fibre

moroccan lamb pizza

2 x 335g (11-ounce) pizza bases with
   tomato paste
600g (1¼ pounds) minced (ground) lamb
1 tablespoon moroccan spice mix
½ cup (140g) greek-style yogurt

1 Preheat oven to 200°C/400°F.
2 Place pizza bases on two oiled oven trays.
3 Cook lamb in heated oiled large frying pan until browned. Add spice mix; cook, stirring, until fragrant. Season to taste.
4 Spoon lamb mixture over pizza bases. Bake, about 10 minutes or until bases are browned lightly.
5 Meanwhile, combine yogurt with 2 tablespoons cold water in small bowl; season to taste.
6 Serve pizzas drizzled with yogurt mixture. Serve sprinkled with fresh coriander leaves if you like.

prep + cook time 30 minutes **serves** 4
nutritional count per serving 21.2g total fat
(7.7g saturated fat); 3227kJ (772 cal);
93.1g carbohydrate; 47.9g protein; 6.7g fibre

lamb sausages with pea mash

1kg (2 pounds) potatoes, chopped coarsely
1 cup (120g) frozen peas
⅔ cup (160ml) buttermilk
8 thick lamb sausages (1.2kg)

1 Boil, steam or microwave potato and peas, separately, until tender; drain. Mash potato; stir in peas and buttermilk. Season to taste.
2 Meanwhile, cook sausages in heated oiled large frying pan.
3 Serve sausages with pea mash.

prep + cook time 25 minutes **serves** 4
nutritional count per serving 78g total fat (36.4g saturated fat); 4393kJ (1051 cal); 39.3g carbohydrate; 43.4g protein; 12.6g fibre

serving suggestion Serve with steamed carrots.
note If you don't have buttermilk, stir 2 teaspoons lemon juice into ⅔ cup (180ml) low-fat milk.

speedy lamb curry

1 large brown onion (200g), chopped finely
⅓ cup (100g) balti curry paste
1kg (2 pounds) diced lamb
410g (13 ounces) canned diced tomatoes

1 Cook onion in heated oiled large saucepan, stirring, until soft and browned lightly. Add curry paste and lamb; cook, stirring, until lamb is browned all over.
2 Add undrained tomatoes and ⅓ cup (80ml) water; bring to the boil. Simmer, covered, about 30 minutes or until lamb is tender. Season to taste.

prep + cook time 50 minutes **serves** 4
nutritional count per serving 24.8g total fat (7.9g saturated fat); 1990kJ (476 cal); 7.8g carbohydrate; 52.8g protein; 4.4g fibre

serving suggestion Serve with steamed basmati rice and fresh coriander leaves.
note Balti curry paste is a medium-hot paste containing coriander, fenugreek and mint, which gives it a distinctive mild "green" flavour.

fetta, basil and vegetable lamb roasts

½ cup (100g) drained char-grilled vegetables,
  chopped coarsely
50g (1½ ounces) fetta cheese, crumbled
2 tablespoons coarsely chopped fresh basil
4 lamb mini roasts (1.4kg)

1 Preheat oven to 220°C/425°F.
2 Combine vegetables, cheese and basil in
small bowl.
3 Make a horizontal cut in each lamb roast to
make a large pocket, without cutting all the way
through. Push vegetable mixture into pockets. Tie
lamb at 3cm (1-inch) intervals with kitchen string.
Place lamb on large oiled oven tray.
4 Roast lamb, uncovered, about 35 minutes. Cover
lamb; stand 10 minutes. Remove kitchen string,
then slice thickly.

prep + cook time 50 minutes serves 6
nutritional count per serving 22.4g total fat
(9.5g saturated fat); 1956kJ (468 cal);
1.2g carbohydrate; 65.2g protein; 0.5g fibre

serving suggestion Serve with a green salad and roast potatoes.

harissa lamb loin chops

¼ cup (75g) harissa sauce
1 tablespoon olive oil
2 tablespoons finely chopped fresh flat-leaf parsley
8 lamb loin chops (800g)

1 Combine harissa, oil, half the parsley and lamb in large bowl.
2 Cook lamb on heated oiled grill plate (or grill pan or barbecue). Serve lamb sprinkled with remaining parsley.

prep + cook time 15 minutes **serves** 4
nutritional count per serving 18.6g total fat (7.1g saturated fat); 1304kJ (312 cal); 3.6g carbohydrate; 32g protein; 0.9g fibre

serving suggestion Serve with a green salad and herbed couscous.
note Harissa is a hot sauce; reduce the amount of harissa used in this recipe according to your taste.

stir-fry hoisin lamb and vegetables

600g (1¼ pounds) lamb strips
⅓ cup (80ml) hoisin sauce
800g (1½ pounds) fresh packaged
  stir-fry vegetables
4 green onions (scallions), sliced thickly

1 Combine lamb and half the sauce in medium bowl. Cover, refrigerate 30 minutes.
2 Stir-fry lamb in heated oiled wok, in batches. Remove from wok.

3 Stir-fry vegetables, half the onion and 2 tablespoons cold water in wok until vegetables are almost tender. Return lamb to wok with remaining sauce; stir-fry until hot.
4 Serve stir-fry topped with remaining onion.

prep + cook time 15 minutes (+ refrigeration)
serves 4
nutritional count per serving 14.7g total fat (4.5g saturated fat); 1651kJ (395 cal); 14g carbohydrate; 47g protein; 9.6g fibre

serving suggestion Serve with steamed rice or stir-fried noodles.

hoisin lamb wraps with cucumber

400g (13 ounces) lamb backstraps
2 tablespoons hoisin sauce
2 lebanese cucumbers (260g)
4 large white soft wraps (170g)

1 Combine lamb with sauce in medium bowl; cover, refrigerate 30 minutes.
2 Cook lamb in heated oiled medium frying pan. Cover lamb; stand 5 minutes then slice thinly.
3 Meanwhile, using vegetable peeler, peel cucumber lengthways into ribbons. Divide cucumber and lamb among wraps; roll to enclose filling.

prep + cook time 15 minutes (+ refrigeration)
makes 4
nutritional count per wrap 8.6g total fat (2.5g saturated fat); 1237kJ (296 cal); 27.3g carbohydrate; 25.9g protein; 2.9g fibre

note Any soft, flat bread is fine; lavash, pitta or mountain bread are all good choices.

warm lamb sausage and ravioli salad

1.2kg (2½ pounds) thick lamb sausages
6 medium tomatoes (900g), chopped coarsely
625g (1¼ pounds) roasted vegetable ravioli
100g (3½ ounces) baby rocket (arugula) leaves

1 Cook sausages in heated oiled large frying pan. Remove from pan, slice thickly; cover to keep warm.
2 Add tomato to pan; bring to the boil. Simmer, uncovered, about 2 minutes or until thickened slightly. Season to taste.
3 Meanwhile, cook ravioli in large saucepan of boiling water until tender; drain.
4 Combine sausages, tomato mixture, ravioli and half the rocket in large bowl. Serve with remaining rocket leaves.

prep + cook time 25 minutes serves 6
nutritional count per serving 54.6g total fat (25.4g saturated fat); 3076kJ (736 cal); 27g carbohydrate; 31.1g protein; 8.7g fibre

pork

italian-style sausage and bean stew

6 pork and fennel sausages (675g)
410g (13 ounces) canned diced tomatoes with
    roasted capsicum
800g (1½ pounds) canned borlotti beans,
    rinsed, drained
¼ cup firmly packed small fresh basil leaves

1 Cook sausages in heated oiled large frying pan.
Remove from pan.
2 Add undrained tomatoes, beans and ⅓ cup
(80ml) water to pan; bring to the boil. Simmer,
uncovered, about 5 minutes or until sauce thickens.
3 Meanwhile, slice sausages thickly; return to pan,
simmer, uncovered, until heated through. Season
to taste.
4 Serve sprinkled with basil. Accompany with
crusty bread, if you like.

prep + cook time 20 minutes serves 4
nutritional count per serving 39.6g total fat
(15.5g saturated fat); 2537kJ (607 cal);
27.5g carbohydrate; 29.8g protein; 11.9g fibre

easy ham

caramelised pineapple and ham pizza

Preheat oven to 220°C/425°F. Peel ½ small pineapple. Slice thinly. Heat oiled large frying pan over high heat. Cook pineapple, both sides, until caramelised. Remove from pan. Place pineapple on two 220g (7-ounce) tomato sauce-topped pizza bases. Top with 220g (7 ounces) sliced leg ham and 1 cup (120g) coarsely grated cheddar cheese. Bake, about 15 minutes or until base is browned and crisp. Cut into wedges to serve.

prep + cook time 25 minutes **serves** 4
nutritional count per serving 17.6g total fat (7.9g saturated fat); 2266kJ (542 cal); 64.2g carbohydrate; 28.1g protein; 5.8g fibre

mini ham and corn quiches

Preheat oven to 200°C/400°F. Whisk 4 eggs and 2 tablespoons water together in large jug; season. Lightly grease two 12-hole (1 tablespoon/20ml) shallow round-based patty pans. Using a 7cm (3-inch) cutter, cut 24 rounds from 3 sheets of shortcrust pastry. Press pastry rounds into pans. Divide 90g (3 ounces) coarsely chopped leg ham and 250g (8 ounces) canned drained corn kernels between pastry cases. Top with egg mixture. Bake about 25 minutes or until quiches are set and pastry is browned lightly.

prep + cook time 40 minutes **makes** 24
nutritional count per quiche 5.8g total fat (2.4g saturated fat); 393kJ (94 cal); 7.6g carbohydrate; 2.7g protein; 0.5g fibre

ham and brie finger sandwiches

Spread 4 slices of wholegrain bread with ⅓ cup
(90g) caramelised onion relish. Top with 125g
(4 ounces) thinly sliced brie cheese and 150g
(5 ounces) sliced leg ham. Top with another 4 bread
slices. Cut crusts from bread, cut each sandwich
into 3 fingers.

prep time 15 minutes **serves** 4
nutritional count per serving 12.4g total fat
(6.9g saturated fat); 1271kJ (304 cal);
29.3g carbohydrate; 17.4g protein; 2.9g fibre

potato rösti with ham and tomato pesto

Coarsely grate 2 medium peeled potatoes (400g).
Drop level tablespoons of potato into oiled large
frying pan; flatten slightly with a spatula. Cook
until base is browned and crisp; turn, cook until
browned. Drain rösti on absorbent paper. Repeat
with remaining potato to make 20 rösti. Top rösti
with 125g (4 ounces) sliced leg ham. Combine
⅓ cup (90g) tomato pesto dip and 1 tablespoon
finely chopped fresh flat-leaf parsley in small bowl.
Top ham with pesto.

prep + cook time 25 minutes **makes** 20
nutritional count per rösti 2.7g total fat
(0.5g saturated fat); 176kJ (42 cal);
2.3g carbohydrate; 1.9g protein; 0.4g fibre

pork cutlets with coriander and fennel salt

4 pork cutlets (940g)
1 teaspoon fennel seeds, toasted
1 teaspoon coriander seeds, toasted
2 teaspoons sea salt flakes

1 Cook pork on heated oiled grill plate (or grill pan or barbecue).
2 Meanwhile, using a mortar and pestle, crush seeds until fine. Add salt, crush lightly to combine. Serve pork sprinkled with fennel salt.

prep + cook time 15 minutes **serves** 4
nutritional count per serving 7.5g total fat (2.5g saturated fat); 798kJ (191 cal); 0g carbohydrate; 30.5g protein; 0g fibre

note Any remaining salt can be used on potatoes, over steamed vegetables or other grilled meats.

portuguese-style skewers

500g (1 pound) pork scotch steaks (neck)
½ cup (125ml) piri piri marinade
½ medium red onion (75g), cut into 8 wedges
1 medium red capsicum (bell pepper) (200g),
  chopped coarsely

1 Cut pork into bite-sized chunks. Combine pork with marinade in medium bowl. Thread pork, onion and capsicum onto 8 bamboo skewers.
2 Cook skewers on heated oiled grill plate (or grill pan or barbecue), brushing with remaining marinade during cooking.

prep + cook time 30 minutes **serves** 4
nutritional count per serving 6.6g total fat (2g saturated fat); 899kJ (215 cal); 8.8g carbohydrate; 28.7g protein; 2.2g fibre

note Soak bamboo skewers in cold water for at least 30 minutes before using to prevent scorching.

sticky pork ribs

2kg (4 pounds) american-style pork spare ribs
1 cup (280g) barbecue sauce
2 tablespoons worcestershire sauce
1 tablespoon dijon mustard

1   Preheat oven to 160°C/325°F. Line large shallow baking dish with baking paper.
2   Cut pork in portions of five or six ribs. Combine sauces and mustard in large bowl; reserve a quarter of the marinade. Add pork to bowl with marinade; turn to coat. Transfer pork to baking dish. Cover dish with foil.

3   Roast pork for 1 hour. Increase oven temperature to 200°C/400°F. Baste pork with reserved marinade. Roast 30 minutes, uncovered, basting occasionally, or until pork is browned and sticky.

prep + cook time 1 hour 45 minutes **serves** 4
nutritional count per serving 17.1g total fat (6.5g saturated fat); 2337kJ (559 cal); 33.3g carbohydrate; 68.3g protein; 1g fibre

serving suggestion Serve with baked potatoes and salad leaves.
note You can ask the butcher to cut the pork into sections for you.

pork meatball curry

600g (1¼ pounds) minced (ground) pork
2 tablespoons mild curry paste
6 medium tomatoes (900g), chopped coarsely
150g (5 ounces) green beans, trimmed, halved

1 Roll level tablespoons of pork into 24 balls. Heat oiled large saucepan over medium heat. Cook meatballs about 5 minutes or until browned all over. Remove from pan. Add curry paste; cook, stirring, until fragrant.
2 Add tomato and ⅓ cup (80ml) cold water; bring to the boil. Simmer, uncovered, stirring occasionally, about 5 minutes or until sauce is thickened slightly.
3 Return meatballs to pan with beans. Simmer, covered, about 10 minutes or until beans are tender. Season to taste.

prep + cook time 35 minutes **serves** 4
nutritional count per serving 15.6g total fat (4.4g saturated fat); 1300kJ (311 cal); 6g carbohydrate; 33.7g protein; 4.9g fibre

serving suggestion Serve with steamed rice.

cheesy ham quesadillas

8 x 15cm (6-inch) white flour tortillas (320g)
⅔ cup (80g) coarsely grated cheddar cheese
250g (8 ounces) sliced leg ham
130g (4 ounces) crumbled fetta cheese

1 Coat base of medium frying pan with cooking oil spray; heat over medium heat. Place 1 tortilla in pan, sprinkle with quarter of the cheddar cheese, quarter of the ham and quarter of the fetta cheese. Top with a tortilla, spray with oil.
2 Cook tortilla in pan, pressing down firmly with a spatula, about 1 minute or until base is browned. Place a plate over frying pan and turn quesadilla onto plate. Slide quesadilla, uncooked-side down, back into pan. Cook 1 minute or until browned. Transfer to plate.
3 Repeat to make three more quesadillas; cut into wedges to serve.

prep + cook time 20 minutes **makes** 4
nutritional count per quesadilla 24.2g total fat (11.7g saturated fat); 2136kJ (511 cal); 42g carbohydrate; 29.5g protein; 2.5g fibre

sesame, ginger and pork stir-fry

440g (14 ounces) pork fillet, sliced thinly
450g (14 ounces) packet flat wide fresh rice noodles
500g (1 pound) baby buk choy, chopped coarsely
½ cup (125ml) sesame, ginger and soy marinade

1 Heat oiled large wok; stir-fry pork, in batches, until cooked through. Remove from wok.
2 Place noodles in medium heatproof bowl, cover with boiling water; separate with fork, drain.
3 Add noodles, buk choy, marinade and 2 tablespoons water to wok. Stir-fry until hot. Return pork to wok; stir-fry until heated through.

prep + cook time 20 minutes **serves** 4
nutritional count per serving 4.6g total fat (1.1g saturated fat); 1158kJ (277 cal); 26.6g carbohydrate; 29.7g protein; 2.9g fibre

serving suggestion Serve with steamed jasmine rice and chopped fresh chilli.

glossary

AÏOLI a homemade garlic mayonnaise that has enflamed the passions of so many people around the world that they hold local aïoli festivals at garlic harvest time.

BAKING PAPER also known as parchment paper or baking parchment – is a silicone-coated paper that is primarily used for lining baking pans and oven trays so cakes and biscuits won't stick, making removal easy.

BEANS
borlotti also called roman beans or pink beans, can be eaten fresh or dried. Interchangeable with pinto beans due to their similarity in appearance – pale pink or beige with dark red streaks.
refried pinto or borlotti beans, cooked twice-soaked and boiled, then mashed and fried, traditionally in lard. A Mexican staple, frijoles refritos (refried beans) are available canned from supermarkets.
snake long (about 40cm), thin, round, fresh green beans, Asian in origin, with a taste similar to green or french beans. Used most frequently in stir-fries, they are also known as yard-long beans because of their length in imperial (pre-metric) measurement.

BREADCRUMBS
fresh bread, usually white, processed into crumbs.
packaged prepared fine-textured but crunchy white breadcrumbs; good for coating foods that are to be fried.
stale crumbs made by grating, blending or processing one- or two-day-old bread.

BUK CHOY also known as bok choy, bak choy, pak choy and chinese white cabbage; has a mild mustard taste. Baby buk choy is smaller, more tender and less peppery than buk choy.

BUTTER we use salted butter unless stated otherwise; 125g is equal to 1 stick (4 ounces).

BUTTERMILK in spite of its name, buttermilk is actually low in fat, varying between 0.6 per cent and 2 per cent per 100ml. Originally the term given to the slightly sour liquid left after butter was churned from cream, today it is intentionally made from no-fat or low-fat milk to which specific bacterial cultures have been added during the manufacturing process.

CAPSICUM also called pepper or bell pepper. Discard seeds and membranes before use.

CHEESE
bocconcini from the diminutive of "boccone", meaning mouthful in Italian; walnut-sized, baby mozzarella, a delicate, semi-soft, white cheese traditionally made from buffalo milk. Sold fresh, it spoils rapidly so will only keep, refrigerated in brine, for one or two days at the most.
brie soft-ripened cow-milk cheese with a delicate, creamy texture and a rich, sweet taste that varies from buttery to mushroomy. Best served at room temperature after a brief period of ageing, brie should have a bloomy white rind and creamy, centre which becomes runny with ripening.
fetta Greek in origin; a crumbly textured goat's or sheep's milk cheese having a sharp, salty taste. Ripened and stored in salted whey; particularly good cubed and tossed into salads.
goat's made from goat's milk, has an earthy, strong taste. Available in soft, crumbly and firm textures, in various shapes and sizes, and sometimes rolled in ash or herbs.
haloumi a Greek Cypriot cheese with a semi-firm, spongy texture and very salty sweet flavour. Ripened and stored in salted whey; best grilled or fried, and holds its shape well on being heated. Eat while still warm as it becomes tough on cooling.
mozzarella soft, spun-curd cheese; originating in southern Italy where it was traditionally made from water-buffalo milk. Now generally made from cow's milk, it's the most popular pizza cheese because of its low melting point and elasticity when heated.
parmesan also called parmigiano; is a hard, grainy cow-milk cheese originating in the Parma region of Italy. The curd for this cheese is salted in brine for a month, then aged for up to 2 years in humid conditions.
pizza cheese a commercial blend of varying proportions of processed grated mozzarella, cheddar and parmesan.
ricotta a soft, sweet, moist, white cow-milk cheese with a low fat content (8.5 per cent) and a slightly grainy texture. The name roughly translates as "cooked again" and refers to ricotta's manufacture from a whey that is a by-product of cheese making.

CHILLI available in many different types and sizes. Use rubber gloves when seeding and chopping fresh chillies as they can burn your skin. Removing seeds and membranes lessens the heat level.
flakes deep-red dehydrated extremely fine slices and whole seeds; good for cooking or for sprinkling over cooked food in the same way as salt and pepper.

CHOY SUM also known as pakaukeo or flowering cabbage; easy to identify with its long stems, light green leaves and yellow flowers. This popular Asian vegetable is eaten, stems and all, steamed or stir-fried.

COCONUT
cream obtained commercially from the first pressing of the coconut flesh alone, without the addition of water; the second pressing (less rich) is sold as coconut milk. Available in cans and cartons at most supermarkets.
desiccated concentrated, dried, unsweetened and finely shredded coconut flesh.
milk not the liquid found inside the fruit, which is called coconut water, but the diluted liquid from the second pressing of the white flesh of a mature coconut (the first pressing produces coconut cream). Available in cans and cartons at most supermarkets.
CORIANDER also called cilantro, pak chee or chinese parsley; bright-green-leafed herb with both pungent aroma and taste. Coriander seeds are dried and sold either whole or ground, and neither form tastes remotely like the fresh leaf.

114

CREAM we used fresh cream, also known as pure or pouring cream unless otherwise stated. Has no additves. Minimum fat content 35%.
thick (double) a dolloping cream with a minimum fat content of 45%.
thickened (heavy) a whipping cream containing thickener. Minimum fat content 35%.

DUKKAH an Egyptian specialty spice mixture made up of roasted nuts, seeds and an array of aromatic spices.

EGGPLANT also called aubergine. Ranging in size from tiny to very large and in colour from pale green to deep purple. Can also be purchased char-grilled, packed in oil, in jars.
baby also called finger or japanese eggplant; very small and slender so can be used without disgorging.

EGGS some recipes in this book may call for raw or barely cooked eggs; exercise caution if there is a salmonella problem in your area, particularly in food to be eaten by children and pregnant women.

FENNEL also known as finocchio or anise; a white to very pale green-white, firm, crisp, roundish vegetable about 8cm-12cm in diameter. The bulb has a slightly sweet, anise flavour, but the leaves have a much stronger taste. Also the name given to dried seeds having a licorice flavour.

FLOUR
plain also known as all-purpose; unbleached wheat flour is the best for baking: the gluten content ensures a strong dough, which produces a light result in baked goods.
self-raising all-purpose plain or wholemeal flour with baking powder and salt added; make it yourself with plain or wholemeal flour sifted with baking powder in the proportion of 1 cup plain flour to 2 teaspoons of baking powder.

HARISSA a Moroccan sauce or paste made from dried chillies, cumin, garlic, oil and caraway seeds. The paste, available in a tube, is very hot and should not be used in large amounts;

bottled harissa sauce is more mild. Available from supermarkets and Middle-Eastern grocery stores

KUMARA the polynesian name of an orange-fleshed sweet potato often confused with yam; good baked, boiled, mashed or fried.

MARINARA MIX a mixture of uncooked, chopped seafood available from fishmarkets and fishmongers.

MINCE MEAT also known as ground meat, as in beef, pork, lamb, veal and chicken.

MUSHROOMS
button small, cultivated white mushrooms with a mild flavour. When a recipe in this book calls for an unspecified type of mushroom, always use buttons.
flat large, flat mushrooms with a rich earthy flavour, ideal for filling and barbecuing. They are sometimes misnamed field mushrooms which are wild mushrooms.
swiss brown also known as roman or cremini. Light to dark brown mushrooms with full-bodied flavour; suited for use in casseroles or being stuffed and baked.

MUSTARD, DIJON also called french. Pale brown, creamy, distinctively flavoured, fairly mild French mustard.

NOODLES, FRESH RICE also called ho fun, khao pun, sen yau, pho or kway tiau, depending on the country of manufacture; the most common form of noodle used in Thailand. Can be purchased in strands of various widths or large sheets weighing about 500g which are to be cut into the desired noodle size. Chewy and pure white, they do not need pre-cooking before use.

PANCETTA an Italian unsmoked bacon, pork belly cured in salt and spices then rolled into a sausage shape and dried for several weeks. Used, sliced or chopped, as an ingredient rather than eaten on its own. Can also be used to add flavour to tough or dry cuts of meat.

PARSLEY, FLAT-LEAFED also known as continental parsley or Italian parsley.

PIRI PIRI PASTE a Portuguese chilli paste made from red chillies, ginger, garlic, oil and various herbs.

PISTACHIOS green, delicately flavoured nuts inside hard off-white shells. Available salted or unsalted in the shell; you can also buy them shelled.

POLENTA also known as cornmeal; a flour-like cereal made of dried corn (maize). Also the dish made from it.

POMEGRANATE MOLASSES has a tart, fruity taste similar to balsamic vinegar. It is available at Middle Eastern food stores, specialty food shops and some delicatessens.

ROCKET also called arugula, rugula and rucola; peppery green leaf eaten raw in salads or used in cooking. Baby rocket leaves are smaller and less peppery.

TOMATOES
canned whole peeled tomatoes in natural juices; available crushed, chopped or diced, sometimes unsalted or reduced salt. Use undrained.
cherry also known as tiny tim or tom thumb tomatoes; small and round.
paste triple-concentrated tomato puree used to flavour soups, stews, sauces and casseroles.
puree canned pureed tomatoes (not tomato paste); substitute with fresh peeled and pureed tomatoes.
semi-dried partially dried tomato pieces in olive oil; softer and juicier than sun-dried, these are not a preserve thus do not keep as long as sun-dried.
sun-dried tomato pieces that have been dried with salt; this dehydrates the tomato and concentrates the flavour. We use sun-dried tomatoes packaged in oil, unless otherwise specified.

WONTON WRAPPERS similar to gow gee or spring roll pastry sheets, made of flour, egg and water, are found in the refrigerated or freezer section of Asian shops and supermarkets.

conversion chart

MEASURES

One Australian metric measuring cup holds approximately 250ml; one Australian metric tablespoon holds 20ml; one Australian metric teaspoon holds 5ml.

The difference between one country's measuring cups and another's is within a two- or three-teaspoon variance, and will not affect your cooking results. North America, New Zealand and the United Kingdom use a 15ml tablespoon.

All cup and spoon measurements are level. The most accurate way of measuring dry ingredients is to weigh them. When measuring liquids, use a clear glass or plastic jug with the metric markings.

We use large eggs with an average weight of 60g.

DRY MEASURES

METRIC	IMPERIAL
15g	½oz
30g	1oz
60g	2oz
90g	3oz
125g	4oz (¼lb)
155g	5oz
185g	6oz
220g	7oz
250g	8oz (½lb)
280g	9oz
315g	10oz
345g	11oz
375g	12oz (¾lb)
410g	13oz
440g	14oz
470g	15oz
500g	16oz (1lb)
750g	24oz (1½lb)
1kg	32oz (2lb)

LIQUID MEASURES

METRIC	IMPERIAL
30ml	1 fluid oz
60ml	2 fluid oz
100ml	3 fluid oz
125ml	4 fluid oz
150ml	5 fluid oz (¼ pint)
190ml	6 fluid oz
250ml	8 fluid oz
300ml	10 fluid oz (½ pint)
500ml	16 fluid oz
600ml	20 fluid oz (1 pint)
1000ml (1 litre)	1¾ pints

LENGTH MEASURES

METRIC	IMPERIAL
3mm	⅛in
6mm	¼in
1cm	½in
2cm	¾in
2.5cm	1in
5cm	2in
6cm	2½in
8cm	3in
10cm	4in
13cm	5in
15cm	6in
18cm	7in
20cm	8in
23cm	9in
25cm	10in
28cm	11in
30cm	12in (1ft)

OVEN TEMPERATURES

The oven temperatures in this book are for conventional ovens; if you have a fan-forced oven, decrease the temperature by 10-20 degrees.

	°C (CELSIUS)	°F (FAHRENHEIT)
Very slow	120	250
Slow	150	300
Moderately slow	160	325
Moderate	180	350
Moderately hot	200	400
Hot	220	425
Very hot	240	475

index

First Published in 2010 by ACP Magazines Ltd,

a division of PBL Media Pty Limited

54 Park St, Sydney

GPO Box 4088, Sydney, NSW 2001.

phone (02) 9282 8618; fax (02) 9267 9438

acpbooks@acpmagazines.com.au; www.acpbooks.com.au

ACP BOOKS

General Manager - Christine Whiston

Associate publisher - Seymour Cohen

Editor-in-Chief - Susan Tomnay

Creative Director & Designer - Hieu Chi Nguyen

Food Director - Pamela Clark

Published and Distributed in the United Kingdom by Octopus Publishing Group

Endeavour House

189 Shaftesbury Avenue

London WC2H 8JY

United Kingdom

phone (+44)(0)207 632 5400; fax (+44)(0)207 632 5405

info@octopus-publishing.co.uk;

www.octopusbooks.co.uk

Printed by Toppan Printing Co., China

International foreign language rights, Brian Cearnes, ACP Books bcearnes@acpmagazines.com.au

A catalogue record for this book is available from the British Library.

ISBN 978 1 74245 063 6 (pbk.)

© ACP Magazines Ltd 2010

ABN 18 053 273 546